# Practice Your Pitch

*21 Lessons from*
*2,500 startup pitches from*
*4 years of leading entrepreneurs at*
*Pitch Practice*

Kevin Sandlin

kevinsandlin.com

**Practice Your Pitch**

Kevin Sandlin is a tech entrepreneur, husband to the girl who put a tack in his seat in the 6th grade, father of two kids adopted from Kazakhstan, and the founder of Pitch Practice, the longest running weekly meetup in the Atlanta startup community. Learn more about Kevin and read his blog at kevinsandlin.com.

Anyone who has ever started anything had to tell someone else about that something. How we communicate what we do is directly related to the success of that effort. Pitch Practice was created to help entrepreneurs improve how they communicate. Pitch Practice is inspired by TED Talks from Simon Sinek and Nancy Duarte, and supported by Atlanta Tech Village and the growing community of entrepreneurs in Atlanta.

This book is for new entrepreneurs who understand that their every word matters and that practicing saying those words is crucial to success.

For my wife of 24+ years, Angel, who had one simple response when I told her I wanted to quit my cushy job at FirstData, start my first business, and have no income for nearly 3 years:

*"Go for it."*

# Table of Contents

PREFACE ......................................................................... 7

INTRODUCTION ............................................................. 9

Chapter 1 - A Brief History of Pitch Practice ..................... 11

Chapter 2 - How Pitch Practice Works ............................... 13

Chapter 3 - Pitch Practice is a Service .............................. 17

Chapter 4 - Practice Makes Perfect .................................. 23

Chapter 5 - The Pitch Practice Methodology ..................... 33

Chapter 6 - Who Are You? You are the Jockey. .................. 47

Chapter 7 - The Problem ................................................. 55

Chapter 8 - Your Solution to the Problem .......................... 71

Chapter 9 - The Customer ................................................ 79

Chapter 10 - The Ask ...................................................... 83

Chapter 11 - Tell Us A Story ............................................ 89

Chapter 12 - Now Grow Your Elevator Pitch ..................... 93

Chapter 13 - The Final Lesson ......................................... 101

Conclusion ..................................................................... 103

APPENDIX: The 21 Lessons ............................................ 105

# PREFACE

**"The will to win is not nearly so important as the will to prepare to win." - Vince Lombardi**

Preparation is the key to success. "Luck" is where preparation meets opportunity. Preparation to communicate means practicing what you are going to communicate. Just as one would prepare to "pop the question", an entrepreneur must prepare to communicate with investors, co-founders, employees, customers, partners, and vendors.

It is the sole responsibility of the leader, the entrepreneur, to communicate the vision of the enterprise, for if he or she cannot communicate the vision - the future - then how can anyone believe in that vision?

Excellent communication is not random. It is not lucky. It is prepared, practiced, perfected over time, like a golf swing, mental toughness, or even a comedy act.

# INTRODUCTION

*"Great leaders must have two things: a vision of the world that does not yet exist and the ability to communicate that vision clearly." - Simon Sinek*

Imagine this hypothetical situation: there are two entrepreneurs, each with the exact same idea, talent, time, cash, timing, and network. Which entrepreneur succeeds and which one fails?

To answer that question, I'll ask another question: how do entrepreneurs gain traction for their idea? Simple answer, they tell people about it. They might use the phone, an ad, a blog, video, podcast, social media, email, or literally tell people on the street. Whatever methods they use to communicate their message, they start with words.

The entrepreneur who communicates better will always be more successful than one who cannot communicate well. Always. It was for this very reason that I created Pitch Practice.

It is that "ability to communicate" that lies at the heart of Pitch Practice. Over the past four and a half years, we have heard thousands of pitches. That experience has led to codifying Pitch Practice down to six simple points and 21 lessons about those points. These points and lessons are the meat of this book.

# Chapter 1 - A Brief History of Pitch Practice

*"You don't have to make your subject and verb agree to serve. You only need a heart full of grace. A soul generated by love." - Martin Luther King Jr.*

In the summer of 2013, I was working on my startup, Deductmor. Deductmor was a mobile app for self-employed individuals to capture all their receipts with their phone camera and insert those expenses into QB or whatever accounting package they used. I wanted to raise some capital, but I had bootstrapped my first 4 startups. In spite of going through an IPO and two acquisitions, I had no idea how to raise money.

While I was on a startup scholarship at Atlanta Tech Village and mentoring entrepreneurs at ATDC, I learned about "Pitch Gauntlet", a monthly meetup led by the principles at Venture Lab at Georgia Tech. I went to Pitch Gauntlet three months in a row, and got clobbered with wisdom every time, but it wasn't enough practice for me to refine my pitch. I asked them if they would consider doing the meetup more often. They politely declined, so I went to the folks at ATV and asked if I could start a weekly meetup group to help me and other entrepreneurs practice our pitches.

On June 27th, 2013, the meetup now known as Pitch Practice was born as "Startup BP", which was a baseball analogy for "taking batting practice." Three weeks after that, we changed the name to Pitch Practice. Two years later, the Village named a conference room "The Pitch Practice Boardroom."

**LESSON 1:** Solve a problem, even if it's just for you at the beginning. You never know who it will help.

# Chapter 2 - How Pitch Practice Works

*"It's the little details that are vital.*
*Little things make big things happen."*
*- John Wooden*

The image below provides a glimpse of how we structure the classic "elevator pitch". This structure isn't the gospel of pitch. You're not going to hell if you don't follow it, but it works.

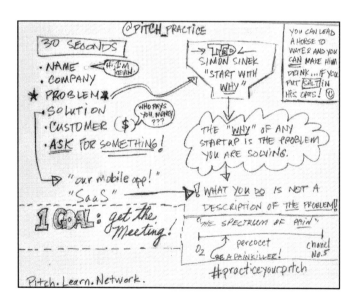

We start with the 30-second pitch, focusing on the problem, as explained in Simon Sinek's TED Talk

"Start with Why." Then we build out to the 3-minute "contest" pitch and then the 5-6 minute investor pitch.

Why do we do it this way? Because it's much easier to start with nothing, build something small, then add to it than it is to start with 20 minutes of death-by-powerpoint and ask, "what can we cut?"

Cut it all and start with the problem you're solving.

## *"80% of success is just showing up." - Woody Allen*

**You just never know**. When I started Pitch Practice, I didn't know if anyone would come to a meetup to pitch your idea to strangers. I still really never know who's going to show up, who's going to pitch, or what they are going to pitch.

Every Friday, I set up in the Pitch Practice Boardroom at ATV, eat some Startup Chowdown lunch, and see who shows up. Sometimes there are 7, and sometimes there are 100.

Is it still a "meetup" if there are only 2 attendees?

Yes, it is. A long time ago, when my wife and I started a community Bible study at our home, we had a lot of back and forth about who'll be there that night and who won't and we sometimes teetered on "should we cancel tonight?"

Then we made the decision that, no matter how many people showed up or didn't show up, we were having Bible study on Tuesday nights at 630PM, period. No more questions, no more IFs. You show up, you get fed (physically and spiritually).

Same goes for Pitch Practice. If one person shows up, we'll add value to their pitch, period.

That has happened on more than one occasion. Once, a student from a local software dev school at ATV showed up, and we chatted for 30 minutes about an idea the student has. He made the same mistake that ever so many people have made before him: he had an idea in search of a problem to solve.

He really struggled to articulate the problem that he could solve, but we eventually got there. He was stoked about this idea when he arrived, and he left even more energized because he had some construct, some context around which to formulate his project. More importantly, he understood how to communicate to others about his idea and the problem that it solves.

**LESSON 2**: be consistent. Show up prepared every time. Because you just never know.

# Chapter 3 - Pitch Practice is a Service

*"A lot of times, people don't know what they want until you show it to them." - Steve Jobs*

I started Pitch Practice to help *me*, and it has become a community vehicle for helping others. That's the "why" of Pitch Practice: *new entrepreneurs don't know how to communicate their value*. When you work from "why" and solve a real problem, you discover innumerable benefits as you do so. I could never have predicted that as an outcome from 4 ½ years (and counting) of Pitch Practice.

**Question**: Work on Weaknesses or Play to Strengths? **Answer**: Yes.

Do a SWOT (Strengths, Weaknesses, Opportunities, Threats) analysis on *you*. Whether you're in a job with a stable company, a full-time entrepreneur, or considering a startup, you have to know your strengths, weaknesses, opportunities, and threats. Specifically, if you're starting a business, you had better know your strengths and weaknesses, and then exercise what you do best and overcome what you do worst.

There are several ways to do both. Here's my list of *what I think* are some of my strengths and weaknesses. I did this exercise in 2014, and it still holds true today.

**Strengths**

1. <u>No fear of failure</u>. I've failed before. It sucks, but life goes on. You figure out how to get to tomorrow, pay the bills, fill that hole, plug that leak, etc. Do I think about failing? Sure, who doesn't? But to me, it's like dying. I don't fear death. I fear dying. Big difference.
2. <u>Leading small teams</u>. I just did kind of an inventory of my weekly schedule, and I realize that I lead, or have a leadership role in, seven small teams.
3. <u>Quick study</u>. There's not much I can't learn, if I want to and if I put my energy into it. I learned product management in 1996 when I had never seen it done before. I learned WiFi. I learned WordPress. I learned just enough

HTML to be dangerous. I've learned crowdsourcing, AWS, Google Apps, and Mechanical Turk. I love to learn and am not afraid of learning something new.

4. <u>I get technology</u>. I can't write code or design a network, but I *get* it, and I can detect BS from the best Systems Engineer and explain why it's BS to the sales and marketing team.

## Weaknesses

1. *Procrastination* - if there's no due date, I will avoid it like the plague until there is a date, then I'll do it.
2. *I can't write code* - I can create an HTML table, but not much more.
3. *I can't sell* - It's the process of sales that I suck at.
4. *I'm terrible at networking* - Introverts unite! Networking events exhaust me.
5. *I tend to get distracted* by the little things.

Naturally, I try as best I can to play to my strengths, and do things I've done well before and know I can do again. As for my weaknesses, those are what drive a couple of things I do on a regular basis, because you can only hide your weaknesses for so long. Eventually, in the pressure of a startup, your strengths will shine and your weaknesses (and those of your team) will be exposed. It's how you overcome these weaknesses that counts.

To overcome my procrastination, I make a list of everything I must get done every day. The list lives until it's all done, even if that's a week from now. I hire salespeople and software developers because even if I learned either or both, I'll never be as good as a professional at either. To overcome my poor networking abilities I do several things, intentionally and purposefully:

1. I run Pitch Practice every week. This meetup has become a regular part of my weekly rhythm, and I've met hundreds of entrepreneurs, investors, and just generally nice and helpful people.
2. I served from the keg at "Atlanta Startup Village" for 3 years. I met every person who came through the door for a beer. I had to.

It's not my natural bent to meet people out of the blue. I'm not the guy who has "never met a stranger." I can't "work a room." I've watched others do it to perfection, but that's not me. To overcome that weakness, I put myself in oncoming traffic, so to speak, and purposely meet everyone I can in that stream of people.

Pitch Practice offers me the opportunity to meet, help, and learn from other entrepreneurs as they practice explaining their business. Filling cups with beer at Startup Village afforded me the pleasure of saying "Hi! How're you!" to 400 people every month.

**LESSON 3:** to overcome your weaknesses, find a way to <u>serve</u> other people as you build those weaknesses into strengths. That's all Pitch Practice ever was or is: a way for me to serve other entrepreneurs by using my strengths and experience. You have strengths and experience, too.

**LESSON 4:** Having a construct in which to create your pitch is crucial. Just like when you start a business, you need some boundaries, a business model, something upon which to base how you go about everything on a day to day basis, you need a place to start and some boundaries around your pitch.

# Chapter 4 - Practice Makes Perfect

## *"Pitching is an acquired skill, not an innate talent, Kawasaki says. It takes practice." - Guy Kawasaki*

I had a great opportunity to speak about Pitch Practice and about pitching in general to a very diverse audience at ROAM Dunwoody. The audience wasn't just tech startups. That got me thinking about "the pitch" in general, and not just as I see it through my tech startup lens.

Everybody – *everybody* – is pitching all the time. Nobody ever thinks about it, much less practices it. But you should. Everyone should practice their pitch. Practicing is part of being prepared, like charging your phone, carrying a pen or your business card. Here are five reasons you must practice your pitch.

1.  You never know who you're going to meet.
2.  You don't want to sound canned, mechanical, or rehearsed.

3. Preparation is the best way to answer opportunity.
4. Everyone loves a good speaker & presentation.
5. You may only get one shot.

At the event at ROAM, I made a strong point that Pitch Practice was created with tech startups in mind, but that the principles of delivering a great elevator pitch, 3-minute pitch, or 5-minute investor deck are the same, no matter who you are or what you're pitching.  Your story must be compelling. Your delivery must be natural. Your call to action must be clear.

Delivering a great pitch or presentation, like anything else in life, requires practice. In front of a mirror, in front of your dog, video recorded on your phone, or with a helpful group like Pitch Practice. No matter how you prepare, you must prepare.

**Always Be Pitching**

Now that you know that you always *are* pitching, you can intentionally always *be* pitching. But first, a haiku about being prepared:

*Frequent travelers*
*have a mantra – A.B.C.*
*Always be charging*

At a recent tech community event, I was reminded of something that we all know we should be always doing, back in the recesses of our minds, but don't often think about.  But we should be thinking about it because to be good at anything means being intentional about it.  At that event, it was clear that one of the presenters had put some serious time, not to mention choreography, into their pitch. They were intentional about their message, their excitement, and their timing (5:00 on the dot).

This thought process is a huge part of Pitch Practice. There were probably about 300+ people at that event. Think of the last networking event you attended. How many people asked you, "So, what do you do?"  How many people did you ask that same question? If you're networking, and you want to be memorable to the people you meet (in a professional way), then you should keep in mind that you *are* always pitching. You're always pitching yourself.  Anytime you tell someone what you do, or what you've done, or what you're planning to do, you are pitching, because you never know who your next employer, client, partner, employee, or investor is going to be.

And, a haiku to complete this thought.

> *All entrepreneurs*
> *Always pitching, all the time*
> *You just never know*

Always be pitching. Intentionally.

**How long should my elevator pitch be?**

A frequent topic of discussion at Pitch Practice is the time for the elevator pitch. Why 30 seconds? Next time you're actually in an elevator, time the ride. It's usually much less than 30 seconds. So why do we base an elevator pitch on that unit of time?

The simple answer is this: you gotta start somewhere. You really don't need 30 seconds to get your message across. We use 30 seconds as an arbitrary tool for building discipline into your words about what it is that you do. But why?

Another simple answer to that question is that, when someone does ask you what you do or what your startup is all about, the last thing you want to do is have them glancing at their watch after you've been blathering on for 3 or 4 minutes. Don't do that.

Limiting your elevator pitch to 30 seconds is about getting your message across succinctly and effectively. Those two just happen to coincide with bring brief. The reason for brevity should be obvious, but to a great number of people, it's not. When you first meet someone or someone asks you a pointed question (e.g., "what's your startup do?"), it's only polite to get to the point, especially where this type of question most often happens: at networking meetings.

Just like we put lines on a field or court, margins on a document, limits on the characters in a tweet, and size optimizations on an image for a social post, it's about discipline. Thirty seconds is completely arbitrary, but the exercise of creating a pattern of words that gets the attention of your listener and compels some action in under 30 seconds is no different than the act of chipping golf balls into a 5-gallon bucket from varying distances.

Practicing your pitch is about learning discipline in your words.

**Time Goes By Quickly**

Time passes so quickly, both in the macro and micro.

In the macro, guess what? It's already _____. How'd that happen? We get busy. We plan each week in minute detail, and plan each weekend with wild abandon so we make sure we don't get to bed on Sunday night and wonder what we did with our weekend. There's basketball season (March Madness! Go Duke!), football season (Go Dawgs!), high school & middle school soccer season, and spring break. And before you know it, you'll be making Memorial Day weekend plans.

In the micro, my Digital Marketing class experienced how fast five minutes passes in harsh reality on "Demo Night", when each student gave a 5 minute (no longer!) presentation of their project.

When I interjected with "one minute!", no fewer than 8 of the students looked at me in horror and said "Wha…? Really??" Five minutes is a really long pitch, but for these new marketers, it was like snapping your fingers.

I asked afterward how many students had practiced their presentations beforehand: *six* out of 17 students had actually said the words and walked through their slides before Demo Night. Those six individuals had experienced how fast time passes when you're up in front of 50 people presenting the work that you have created.

Others were very prepared. On at least 3 occasions, when I said "one minute", the presenters looked at me and quietly said, "OK," and clicked on their "Thank you / Q&A" slide. Boom.

Whatever you're doing, if you're going to be timed, you would do well to practice before the real deal.

**You'll never say it like that in real life!**

One of the biggest "objections" (put in quotes because it usually comes across as a look-down-mynose derogatory comment) to "practicing your pitch" that I've heard is this:

### *"You're never going to say that in real life!"*

We practice saying the elevator pitch over and over and over, ad nauseam, until we get it "right." But it's true. You never will say it exactly like you do at Pitch Practice. Here are some other things you will never, ever do.

- You'll never juggle a soccer ball on your feet, thighs, shoulders, and head 100 times during a real soccer game.
- You'll never hit a 7-iron 50 straight times from the same spot aiming at the same target in a real golf tournament.
- You'll never take 25 three-pointers from the same spot on the floor with no defense in a real basketball game.
- You'll never hit a tackling dummy in a real football game.
- You'll never hit 100 straight serves in a real tennis match.
- You'll never juggle a baseball on the bat in a real game.

- You'll never spin a basketball on your finger in a real game.
- You'll never deliver a 5-minute investor deck without interruptions, questions, or comments from real investors.

The more you do something – *anything* – the better you get at doing that thing. So, no, you will never shake hands with a complete stranger and then proceed through a canned, rehearsed elevator pitch. You will, however, give an answer to "so, what do you do?" or "what's your startup do?"

Are you ready to give that answer? Have you practiced saying the words in front of real people who are not afraid to hurt your feelings and give you real, objective feedback? That's what we do at Pitch Practice every week, and that's where you can practice the words you're going to deliver when someone asks you, "So, what do you do?"

So, next time you're swinging away with that 7-iron, consider how much confidence that practice gives you on the course and apply that same strategy to how you articulate what you do.

**LESSON 3**: Practice makes perfect. Get so comfortable with your pitch that you don't sound canned. That takes time. Until you say it out loud, in front of actual people, you never know how it's going to sound.

**LESSON 4:** Until you stand up and do it in front of real people, you don't know that your hands never came out of your pockets or that you sway back and forth or never look at anyone.

# Chapter 5 - The Pitch Practice Methodology

## *"People don't buy what you do, they buy why you do it." - Simon Sinek*

When I started Pitch Practice in June of 2013, I didn't know what it would eventually be or what value it might have to others. It was simply a fun gathering of fellow entrepreneurs to help each other answer the question, *"So, what do you do?"* a little better, and also help us prepare for events like Atlanta Startup Village or Startup Riot or any of the dozens of pitch contests that seem to keep popping up. The weekly event certainly has accomplished all those goals.

However, it wasn't until running the meeting for a more than eighteen months that I found two TED talks that completely changed the way I lead Pitch Practice, and the way I help startup entrepreneurs (a) develop their elevator pitch and (b) tell their story.

- Simon Sinek, *"How Great Leaders Inspire Action"*
- Nancy Duarte, *"The secret structure of great talks"*

In developing a 30-second elevator pitch, I developed the pitch practice structure, and have used it in every pitch talk since.

A slightly deeper explanation:

1. Your Name
2. Your Organization (if you have one yet)
3. **The Problem you're solving**
4. Your Solution to that problem
5. Customer (who will pay you money?)
6. Ask - what do you need?

There's no right or wrong order, and you don't have to use all these elements if you don't want to, but this is a place to start, a structure, a set of boundaries that will help you get from a blank piece of paper to a very short and eloquent elevator pitch that you can say to anyone and they'll get it.

## Focus on the Problem

"Problem" is in **bold** above because that's where your focus should be if you're starting a tech business today. We get this structure from the *Lean Startup Methodology*, codified by Eric Ries and Steve Blank. The basic tenet is that you don't come up with great ideas. Rather, you create solutions to really big expensive problems. So, if you're not solving a painful market problem, you might want to re-evaluate your idea.

Your focus in your 30-second pitch should be 99% on articulating the problem. When you're talking to your proper target audience, they will all "get it" because they are living with that problem today (that's how you know they are your proper target audience), and they will immediately want to know more about your solution.

That gets us to the first TED talk that inspires Pitch Practice (sorry it took so long), in which Simon Sinek brilliantly explains that people don't buy your "what" they buy your "why". Sinek refers to Apple as one of the examples of how a brand can be so good at their "why" that it doesn't matter what their "what" actually is. Why would you buy a music player or a phone or a watch from a computer company?

Because you know it will break all the previously defined boundaries, just like the Macintosh did in 1984, the iPod did in 2001, the iPhone in 2007, the iPad in 2010, and maybe the iWatch in 2015, or the Apple HomePod in 2018.

## Start With Why

In your pitch, the problem you are solving is your "why", and is the focus of all your energy and words. When you can simplify a huge market problem into just a few words so that your 5-year-old kid or your 85-year-old grandmother understands it, then you truly understand it and can convey your vision for solving that problem to anyone.

Too often, great ideas are presented by entrepreneurs who have no desire, preparation, or structure for telling their story, so the problem goes unsolved until a "visionary" who can focus on the "why" enters the market.

# *"If you can't explain it simply, you don't understand it well enough." - Albert Einstein*

The second TED talk involves actually telling your story in a pitch much longer than 30 seconds, and is a bit more complex, but incredibly powerful when utilized properly. Part of Apple's amazing success is the ability of its founder, Steve Jobs, to keep his audience on pins and needles. Nancy Duarte takes a deep look at the speech Jobs gave in introducing the iPhone in 2007 and Martin Luther King, Jr.'s "I have a dream" speech. She dissected both speeches so thoroughly as to bring out a purposeful and powerful pattern that keeps the audience thoroughly engaged and on the edge of their seats.

The pattern itself is simple: down and up and down and up and down. But what does that mean to the entrepreneur pitching his or her startup to an audience? It really is simple, and yet so powerful.

This simple pattern of carrying the audience to new highs and new lows one after the other has an amazing effect on the listeners, mainly by keeping them thoroughly engaged until the peak of the speech in which the solution is shared and the vision cast.

I had listened to and offered suggestions for hundreds of pitches from all kinds of markets and entrepreneurs, but until I heard and applied Sinek and Duarte's TED Talks to Pitch Practice, everything was based on nothing other than, "that seems to work better".

Having a structure to anything makes it so much simpler to begin, and having a structure to your pitch and your story can carry your startup a long way towards success.

## Pitch Practice is a Starting Point

Over the years of Pitch Practice, we've heard the following phrase quite a bit: "I'm not really sure where to start." It's common, and it's ok. One of the best tools to come out of these past 3 years that really helps new entrepreneurs is the construct that we provide from which anyone can create a great pitch.

Having a construct in which to create your pitch is crucial. Just like when you start a business, you need some boundaries, a business model, something upon which to base how you go about everything on a day to day basis, you need a place to start and some boundaries around your pitch.

Given a green field and an open mic, most people tend towards launching into a lengthy explanation of *what they do*. While that can be impressive at times, it always leaves the audience asking, "Uh, so what's that got to do with me?" Your pitch is not about *you*. Your pitch is about the group of people for whom you provide a service, namely the service of solving some problem or other. Your target audience - *not you* - should be the star of the show.

That's where the construct that has come from 2,000+ pitches focuses: the problem. Inspired by Sinek's TED Talk, book, and subsequent movement, the "why" of a startup is the problem that the startup is solving.

It's pretty simple. I've worn out the line, "*It's not the gospel. You're not going to Hell if you don't use it, but it works.*" So, I'll stick with it. Pitch Practice is a starting point. Some of the best pitches we've ever heard barely touch this construct, and it certainly does not have to be in any particular order.

It's what works best for you and your audience. What you say best, what rolls off the tongue the best, and what gets your message across to your audience most effectively. The six points of the Pitch Practice methodology are a starting point, nothing more.

**Boil it down**

OK, so you have this idea, and you've talked to everyone and their mother-in-law about it, and it's starting to make some sense…to *you*. Remember, you were wrong the first time, right? Then you were wrong again the second and third times, right? It's ok. Anyone who has ever started a business and seen it through to the bitter end (good, bad, or ugly) has been wrong at least once, and those instances of being completely wrong are worth several slides in their speaking engagements. But now you've got your arms around this thing, right?

Now boil it down. Simplify it. Say it so your 4-year-old or your grandmother *gets it* and can easily tell anyone they know about your nutso idea. Can't do it? Then you don't understand it yet yourself.

Here's a simple exercise that we teach at Pitch Practice to help the holders of new ideas boil them down. Ask yourself the following questions:

1. What's the problem you're solving?
2. What's your solution to the problem?
3. Who will pay for your solution?

Let's use red-hot Atlanta startup *Calendly* as an example.

- **What's the problem?** Emailing back and forth and back and forth trying to find a good time to meet with someone is time-consuming and tedious. We've all done this before.
- **What's Calendly's solution to the problem?** *"Calendly helps you schedule meetings without the back-and-forth emails."* Notice there's nothing about <u>how</u> they do it?
- **Who will pay for it?** People and teams who schedule appointments or arrange meetings.

Did I get those answers right? Can you repeat that in 30 seconds? If so, then you understand, and can repeat and pitch Calendly's business. Now, what about yours?

Boil it down. The boiled down explanation becomes the skeleton of your elevator pitch. Memorize it so it rolls off your tongue like the Pledge of Allegiance.

## The First Step Towards Creating A Great Pitch

In 2015 and 2016, I taught 60+ classes and workshops for General Assembly about social media, Google Analytics, WordPress blogging, digital marketing, marketing technology, and various other topics. At the beginning of most of these sessions, everyone asked, *"Do I need my computer?"*

There are 2 reasons that attendees ask this question. First, will they need their computer to actually complete any specific tasks? Second, will they need their computer to take notes? The first one is easy. The second question is a personal preference, but that preference comes with some science. If you take notes by typing, you're putting yourself at a disadvantage, because when you write something down, you remember it better.

The same type of science applies to when you are creating something new. Writing down your goals makes them "real". Writing someone a personal "Thank You" note really ups your relationship game. Writing down your tasks enables you to check them off one by one, bringing a Dave Ramsey sense of accomplishment. Also, when you see a word written down, that sight evokes new thoughts about that word, its meaning to you, and its context. Finally, when you write something down, the very act of writing it down seals it in your memory **7X better** than seeing it, hearing it, or typing it.

As you've probably guessed by now, the first step towards creating a great pitch for your business or startup is to write it down. Specifically, write down the following points:

1. What is the **problem** your organization is solving?
2. What is your **solution** to this problem?
3. Who is your most ideal **customer**?

4. What do you **need** today to succeed in
   solving the problem?

It's vitally important for you, the founder & leader,
to know and understand each of these points each in
its most intimate detail. How else will you impart
this knowledge to employee number 1 or employee
100? It's your torch to carry, and you are the one
who will communicate these answers to anyone and
everyone.

An additional step that I find very helpful for this
exercise is to answer each question in the form of,
or at least in the length of, a tweet: 140 characters
only (#oldschool). Einstein said, "If you cannot
explain it simply, you do not understand it well
enough." I agree wholeheartedly! You should be
able to explain what you do to a 5-year-old and your
grandmother at the same time, and have both of
them generally "*get it*."

Doing so requires brevity and simplicity. It's not
easy, but that's why we practice, and practice begins
with the first time you write it down.

**LESSON 5:** You really don't need 30 seconds to
get your message across. We use 30 seconds as an

arbitrary tool for building discipline into your words about what it is that you do. Set your own bar for excellence, then practice and beat it.

# Chapter 6 - Who Are You? You are the Jockey.

## *"Properly understood, any new and better way of doing things is technology." - Peter Thiel*

If you ask 10 of the top 10 venture capital firms or 10 of the top 10 tech startup accelerators in the US what their #1 criterion is for investing in or betting on a startup, you'd get a pretty consistent answer: *"We bet on the jockey, not the horse."* Team, team, team.

It's <u>all</u> about the founding team. With that knowledge, it's critical to include some nugget of information about you or your team in your pitch. Of course, everyone's experience is different, so there's more than one way of injecting your team's experience into an elevator pitch.

Here are some ideas that line up with the Pitch Practice methodology of constructing your elevator pitch, based on the background of Shane Ballman, the founder and CEO of SynapseMX, a 500Startups graduate and early Pitch Practice attendee.

- **Name** – when you introduce yourself, it's easy to include a short story, such as, "During my 15 years of managing airplane maintenance at Southwest Airlines…"
- **Problem** – introduce your experience by explaining how you discovered, validated, or solved the problem you are addressing: "After enduring this issue for 15 years in the airline maintenance space, I began building a team to create a solution to the problem."
- **Solution** – how did you come up with your solution? Most of the time, the solution is born out of experiencing the problem. "Our team has a total of 85 years of experience in the airline maintenance space, and we've solved the problem."
- **Customer** – If you've lived the problem, validated the problem, and solved the problem, you almost assuredly know exactly who your target customer is, based on your experience: "We've all worked in the airline industry for 10+ years each, so we have

significant relationship equity with our customer base."

- **Ask** – Sometimes, your experience can be your strength, but it can also help you identify a need in your team. "Our founding team is made up of airline maintenance engineers with dozens of years of experience. We're actively seeking out enterprise sales professionals with 5+ years of experience in complex sales to the airline industry."

There are lots of ways of sharing your team's experience, and no two will ever be the same; however, your team's experience is directly related to the chances of success for your startup. Experienced investors will base their evaluation of your startup, at least in part, on the experience of your team.

If you and your team do not have any experience, that does not disqualify you from success at all, but you would be wise to own it up front. VC and accelerators can smell BS a mile away, and if you're 22 or 23 years old, experience may not be your best asset. Own that up front and get it out of the way by focusing on your talent, energy, and your ability to learn from your advisors.

Trying out different ways to deliver your pitch is the reason Pitch Practice exists in the first place. As the folks at FirstRound recently said, *"Practice is critical, and it's the part of the process that is the most easily overlooked, procrastinated and underutilized."* Every time you practice your pitch, you learn something new, and every new pitch you hear, you learn something new that you can apply (or avoid!) in your own pitch.

**Someone has already stolen your idea**

It hasn't happened in quite a while, but at the Pitch Practice meetup, it used to be a fairly regular occurrence. Someone would attend, but say nothing until the final call of "ok, who else would like to practice their pitch?" They'd invariably speak up with something like the following:

> *"I really want to do my pitch, but we haven't signed any sort of NDA and you (speaking to*

*me, the meetup leader) haven't said anything
about confidentiality or non-competition."*

That's when it would get kind of awkward until I
learned how to handle this exact situation. It's not
difficult, meaning the words I use are simple and
straightforward; however, the person who brought
up this objection to sharing their pitch has sincere
trepidations about sharing their idea. That needs to
be taken seriously because most of the time they
have an experiential reason for not sharing more
openly.

They've probably been burned before. I think we all
know how that feels. I know I do. You share
something that you're really excited about with
someone you trust, and then a few weeks, months,
or years later, you learn that person you trusted has
taken your idea and run with it. They stole your
idea.

That's a real thing. It happens. All the time. So, we
need to be respectful of that person's experience and
fear of being burned again.

But that does not change the truth of the matter, and that truth is: **Anyone can steal - and most likely already has stolen your idea. But nobody can steal your execution.**

When you have an idea, you and you alone carry the vision for that idea and how it will look and work itself out over the next 1, 2, 5, 10 years. That's *YOUR* vision, and nobody else can see it or execute on it. That's your advantage. Sometimes, that might be your *only* advantage. Therefore, share your idea.

Someone has (more than likely) already stolen it! They just call it something different and you don't know about it yet. That's what we call "competition", and competition is good. Competition makes us work harder to be better to set ourselves apart and move toward that vision.

Pitch Practice is all about practicing so you can get better. If you cannot articulate what you're doing, it's going to be very difficult to get co-founders, partners, investors, or customers. If you need to get an NDA from everyone you talk to, how will you ever get any feedback on whether or not your idea is good or bad?

**LESSON 6:** If you have deep domain expertise, say it! That means you've lived this problem, and you understand who it affects the results of fixing that problem. It means you have credibility.

**LESSON 7:** Anyone can steal your idea. Nobody can steal your execution. So, share your idea. Someone already has stolen it! They just call it something different and you don't know about it yet. If you have to get an NDA from everyone you talk to, you're doomed from the start.

# Chapter 7 - The Problem

## *"Success is not delivering a feature; success is learning how to solve the customer's problem." - Eric Ries*

In both Pitch Practice and in my work with my content marketing clients, one of the most challenging tasks is nailing down the problem statement. Almost every time I ask the question at Pitch Practice, "what is the problem that [*insert startup name here*] is solving?" the answer I get is a good description of what the startup *does*.

> *What your startup does is not the same thing as the problem your startup is attempting to solve.*

Again, we go back to three resources that have greatly helped me in leading Pitch Practice as well as mentoring startup entrepreneurs and pitching my own ventures:

- The Lean Startup – We don't start businesses with great ideas. We start businesses to solve a big, nasty, hairy, stinking problem in an industry we know.

- Start with Why – Your "why" is the problem you're solving…the problem that you know about, have lived with, understand, and can solve.
- The secret structure of great talks – Telling a great story is a science, and there is a story behind how you arrived at your solution to this great big problem.

These same things *again*?!? Yes. A very wise mentor of mine says often, "Good communication is consistent and repetitive. Good communication is consistent and repetitive." We have Pitch Practice *weekly* for this very reason.

Now, from each of these fantastic resources and the combination of the three, the entrepreneur can now (a) come up with a great business idea, (b) understand how to create a marketing message as well as craft a solid pitch, and (c) learn how to craft a great story around the business.

With those arrows in your quiver, let's take on the problem statement. Here are five characteristics of the problem statement:

1. **It's not about *you***, Mr. Serial Entrepreneur with all kinds of great ideas.
2. It's about your target customer, **their pain or their problem** or their obstacle in life or in business.
3. It's a description of **something that is broken**, inefficient, old or obsolete.
4. It's your **reason for existing** as a startup (you're not a "business" yet)
5. It's something you've lived in or around for a significant period of time (**domain expertise**)

With the understanding of these 5 characteristics of the problem, you now have some boundaries within which to work to create a great problem statement that will instantly grab your audience's attention. Your articulation of the problem will hit home with your audience (the *right* audience) because they, too, have lived with the pain of this problem for years.

Use this construct when you set out to develop your problem statement. That's where everything starts. If there's no problem statement, there's no business.

## Focus on the Problem

Since we now agree that good communication is consistent and repetitive, it's ok to keep teaching the same things over and over. Every week at Pitch Practice we listen to a dozen or so pitches from new entrepreneurs about new ideas. We start with (a reminder of) the simple method of developing your 30-second pitch:

- Your name
- Your company name (if you have one yet)
- What's the problem you are solving
- What's your solution
- Who is your customer (who pays you money?)
- What do you need (aka the ask)?

This Pitch Practice structure is an arbitrary method. There's no science behind it, other than it works as a basic structure for learning how to pitch your idea, your company, your product, or even *you* if you're seeking employment or contract work. You don't have to work in the above order, and sometimes it's actually more effective to say your name *last* so that piece will be more easily remembered.

In using this structure, two things invariably happen:

1. People get the solution confused with the problem
2. People have difficulty figuring out how to state the problem briefly, personally, and in a manner that causes the audience to "get it" immediately.

The first issue is really one of semantics. I ask, *"What's the problem XYZ startup is solving?"*, and someone always responds with a really good description of what XYZ startup *does*, but not what the problem is. The two are very different. See if you can describe the problem, rather than what the company does (or intends to do), because the best thing any new startup can do is solve a big problem.

My suggestion to anyone who stumbles here is this: **focus on the problem**. Chris Turner of Ten Rocket nailed this early on with a real problem, especially in Atlanta. His pitch went something like this:

*"Entrepreneurs have great ideas, but those ideas rarely make it to the MVP."*

He's adjusted it since he started Ten Rocket, mainly because his MVP-building startup has had so much success, but the core remains the same. He focused on the problem, and in doing so left the solution in the eyes and ears of the audience. Anyone and everyone in the Atlanta tech startup community knows and can usually relate to the problem of having a great idea but not being a software developer and not being able to find an available software developer to be a co-founder. It's a huge problem!

**It's not you. It's me.**

I once led an all-day seminar at General Assembly in Atlanta. This class was a 6-hour event in which we compressed the 60 hours of the General

Assembly Digital Marketing class down to 6 hours, with lunch from Chipotle included.

The event had some challenges: the Ponce City Market power went out on Friday night, leaving us with no air conditioning all day Saturday. In July. In Atlanta. You heard that right. It reached 80 degrees in our classroom, but the many oscillating fans and ice cream sandwiches and popsicles made us feel loved anyway.

So, we used this actual, physical problem to discuss the first aspect of digital marketing: branding. One of the most visible aspects of your brand is your message. What you say matters. Every word matters, because your brand is everything you do. We used a simple exercise to demonstrate the point that every word matters. Here's that simple exercise.

*Answer each of these 4 questions in the form of a tweet, using 140 characters (#oldschool) or less. Add an image if you like, if that helps illustrate your brand, but the 140 characters should also stand alone.*

*1. What are your core values?*

2. *What industry or market problem are you solving?*
3. *Who is your optimal customer and how do you reach them?*
4. *Describe your business.*

It's a good way to find out (a) *if* you know your brand and (b) how *well* you know your brand. We walk through this exercise because if you, as the founder or entrepreneur or brand ambassador don't know your brand, how can you communicate that brand to anyone else, inside or outside the company?

We start with the second part of this exercise: "what is the industry or market problem you are solving?" In creating this little exercise, the inspiration for this step is - wait for it! - Simon Sinek's 2009 TED Talk and book, *"Start with Why."*

The class did this exercise, taking about 15 minutes to create the 4 tweets. Where we ran into the most trouble was this step number 2. It is a trend: *entrepreneurs have great difficulty distinguishing the problem statement from the description of their business.* In other words, when I ask "what problem are you solving?" the answer I get most often is *"we do this and that, creating value here and there and saving our customers time and money with these benefits,"* and then they proceed to list all the benefits.

**This answer is completely wrong, and it starts with the first word, "we".**

The problem you are solving has absolutely nothing to do with "we" or "us" or "I" or "me". The problem you are solving is a problem out in the market that your customer has. When you are talking to a potential customer and that customer hears (ad nauseam) what *you* do, you've lost them. When you start with the problem that *your customer has every day* (start with why), you make a friend. They now know that you see and understand their problem. And, most importantly, that you solve that problem.

## *"It's not you. It's me." - Seinfeld, The Lip Reader, Season 5, Episode 6*

When you're stating your problem, remember "it's not you, it's me", and "me" is your customer. It's all about the customer's problem. Your problem statement has nothing to do with you. Rather, it's why you exist. Start with why. Start with the problem, and solve it.

## Defining the problem is very hard

Every week at Pitch Practice, we go through a simple exercise with every pitch. After the entrepreneur delivers his or her pitch, I ask *the group* the following questions, to see how well the message of the pitch was received. As you can see, these questions simply affirm the six points of the Pitch Practice structure.

1. What is his/her name?
2. What is the organization name?
3. What is the problem they are trying to solve?
4. Who is the customer?
5. What is their solution?
6. What did they ask for?

Generally, these are pretty easy questions to answer; however, the point of asking these questions *of the audience* (the pitching entrepreneur is not allowed to answer unless we get stuck) is to determine if, and how well, the speaker's message got through.

Most of the time, we get stuck on two or three of these points for various reasons. But one question gets people tripped up every single week: *what is the problem they are trying to solve?*

Without fail, when we ask this question, someone will answer it with an accurate description of what the startup does, and they are completely wrong. What the startup or business does is not a description of the problem. My go-to line here is this:

> ***"if you use the words I, me, my, we, our, or us in your description of the problem, you are wrong."***

The problem you are solving – your "why" for creating your startup – is not you (hopefully). You are providing the solution. The problem is out there in the marketplace. For example, people used to use spreadsheets to keep track of thousands of customers, contacts, messages, and orders. Or, hailing a cab, riding in a cab, paying for a cab, and dealing with a nasty cab driver is a bad experience. Or, there are no hotel rooms in SFO during DreamForce and I use my vacation home for exactly

2 weeks each year and the rest of the time it sits empty.

Those are all problem descriptions that have nothing to do with Salesforce, Uber, or Airbnb. Those companies solve those problems with their products and services. The problem is the pain in a market space. Your solution is what you do to solve it. You must know - and very clearly articulate - that difference to your audience.

## How big is the problem?

The problem you are solving is your reason for being. It's your "why", and you should, if at all possible, weave a story about how you came to know about, experience, and come to a solution to this problem. But you should also work to demonstrate the relative size of the problem. That's what's known as the "Total Addressable Market" (TAM).

In other words, how big a problem is this thing you're tackling?

That's a tough piece of information to know, and even tougher to slip into an elevator pitch. But it needs to be done. First, you need to know the size of your market before you set out to build a business around it. Is it even big enough to support a lifestyle business or a growth startup? How do you know? That's the type of information that comes naturally from having lived, or experienced, the problem first hand.

Second, you need to figure out a way to put that number or set of numbers into your pitch. Here are some examples from pitches we've heard at Pitch Practice.

- "Every 30 seconds a bike is stolen in the U.S., and the average cost of a bike is $400."
- "66% of millennials have student loan debt, and the average debt is $35,000."
- "60% of millennials are leaving their jobs because they are not getting the leadership development that they want."

Each of these – in one sentence or maybe 3 seconds – gives a solid look at the size of the market. Now, if you're talking to an investor, that investor may or may not have an interest in that market, but you'll get to that point much quicker when you demonstrate that you know the problem and the size of the market. One of the worst things you can do is deliver a compelling pitch, and then not be able to back it up with real-world data.

The total addressable market (TAM) belongs in every pitch. If possible, use actual numbers that you've discovered in your research, rather than "I firmly believe" or "I feel that", because those phrases don't mean anything. In fact, using such phrases will quickly demonstrate to investors that you have no idea what you're talking about and that you haven't done any homework.

If you don't know the size of your addressable market, learn it first, before you pitch.

**LESSON 8**: The problem is the pain in a market space. Your solution is what you do to solve it. You must know the difference.

**LESSON 9:** You have competition. Don't ever say "we have no competition" anywhere in your pitch, or anywhere else for that matter. Your biggest competitor is *status quo*, and getting people to change the way they do things is incredibly hard. If you really, actually don't have any competition, you have discovered something far bigger than you know, or there is no market for other competitors to enter.

# Chapter 8 - Your Solution to th    /

*"You cannot be sure you really understand any part of any business problem unless you go and see for yourself firsthand. It is unacceptable to take anything for granted or to rely on the reports of others." - Eric Ries*

Now that you've found a big, nasty problem in a large market, and you can articulate that problem so that every head in the room nods as your audience "gets it", it's time to put words to your solution.

You learn about the problem you're solving through customer discovery, before you ever build anything that smells like a product or service, by asking hundreds of people in the targeted market (usually the space in which you have at least some domain expertise) and finding out what their daily pain is. Here's a great example from Atlanta's startup community.

- MailChimp – Creating and sending an email newsletter is horribly complicated and confusing, and the email service provider software UIs are awful.

Do you know what the solution is? You can probably figure it out from the problem statement, because MailChimp was started from the recognition of a bad problem in a large market space. But their idea for a business was not what came first. The problem came first. MailChimp was created to solve the problem. The solution became the business.

After going to such pains to articulate the problem you're solving, how do you articulate your solution?

## Don't Give Away The Store In Your Pitch

"You can lead a horse to water, but you can't make him drink," right? Nope. A *lie from the pit of hell*.

That's right, you've been told a lie for a long, long time. I'll explain shortly. For now, consider your elevator pitch. You've got a maximum of 30 seconds, assuming you have the full attention of your audience. What can you say in that time? Better question: what *should* you say?

Before you answer that using the tried and true construct as the starting point for your pitch, consider this: what is the goal of the elevator pitch? To get the sale? No. To get an investment? No. The elevator pitch has one goal and only one goal:

### *To get the next meeting*.

With that understanding, what should you say in your elevator pitch to accomplish your singular goal? Hint: *not the whole enchilada*. You only have 30 seconds and one goal, and you now know that you must focus on the problem. That should narrow the focus of your words quite well, down to just enough to get your audience interested. At a recent session of Pitch Practice, angel investor Charlie Paparelli made a very interesting comment:

> *"A good test of an elevator pitch is if it results in a meaningful discussion afterward."*

Brilliant! In other words, your elevator pitch should be the spark, not the flamethrower, howitzer, or B52. Your pitch should get your audience talking, get them interested, whet their appetite for more. Your elevator pitch should get you to the next meeting.

Now, about that thirsty horse. If you put salt in the horse's oats, he will drink when you get him to the water. Your pitch is the salt in the oats of your audience. Make them thirsty for more.

### Are you "Uber for this" or "Match.com for that"?

It's not easy to get your full message across in a short elevator pitch. You want to make a great first impression, and you want to make sure your audience "gets it". But what if you have a really complex offering or your market space is not really well known?

To help get over that hurdle, it may help to think of an analogy (or three) that enables your listeners to easily understand what it is that you're doing. No analogy is perfect, but many times using the right analogy can very quickly get your message across, especially to your target audience. Here are some simple examples.

- Blockbuster video through the mail (Netflix)
- Email for sending someone money (PayPal)
- Lightweight MS Office in a browser (Google Apps)

Those might help the thought process of coming up with an analogy that describes your business idea. From recent sessions of Pitch Practice, here are some of the analogies that have been used effectively.

- LinkedIn for professional soccer players (Arenalinq)
- Uber for valet parking (Luxe)
- A coding boot camp for marketing technology (DGM Camp)

Your business is like *something*, so if you're having trouble explaining what you do, try to find a good, popular analogy that will help anyone understand your business. Not every business has a nice analogy and not every pitch requires an analogy. And one should be careful when applying analogies, especially when you think you might use "Uber for X". That one has been used in every conceivable way in this new sharing economy.

## Remember the KISS Principle

If you've clearly articulated the problem to the correct audience, then describing your solution can and should be very simple. Just say what your solution is:

- Software
- A mobile app
- A website
- A device
- A service
- A community
- Software as a Service

Think back a few pages to the Calendly example: *schedule meetings without the back-and-forth emails.* The very next question will be, "OK, how do you do that?" Next meeting, please.

Whatever your solution is, just say *what it is*, but stay away from describing HOW it works to solve the problem. Remember, salt in oats. Focus on the problem. Say the solution. Get the next meeting.

**LESSON 10**: If there's a simple analogy you can use (e.g., "match.com for networking"), use it. Sometimes that's what makes it clear or real for your audience. However, be careful using "Uber for _____." That can backfire on you in a hurry.

# Chapter 9 - The Customer

## *"Get out of the building" - Steve Blank*

Point number six in the Pitch Practice method of developing your pitch is "who is the customer?" We put this piece of information in the elevator pitch because, right after articulating the problem that you are solving, knowing your customer is the next most important piece of information that you can convey to your audience.

After we've identified a problem somewhere in a marketplace, the next thing we do is get out of the building, talk to as many potential customers as we can, and validate the problem. The Lean Startup calls this process *customer discovery*. It's not selling, because you don't have a product to sell yet.

Customer discovery is literally discovering who the customer is and what they need and how they go about acquiring products and services. The customer is the entity that is experiencing the problem that you have identified, validated, and solved (or are in the process of solving). That entity will pay you money for your product or service at some point.

## "Everyone" is not a customer

Just as important as being ridiculously specific about the problem you're solving is being ridiculously specific about who your customer is, especially early on in the life of your business. It may well be that the entire world could be your target audience, but when you're a 1 or 2 or 3 person startup, you can't market to, sell to, or support the whole world. Even Facebook started with a very specific user in mind: college students at Harvard. But let's not get confused here. There are customers and there are *users*. Customers pay you money. Users don't. Facebook has 2+ billion users, but we don't pay them money. Facebook's advertisers pay them money.

At some point, someone has to pay your startup money, or you won't survive. Very, very few startups can be like Instagram (2 years old, 10 employees, zero revenue, sold to Facebook for $1 Billion), and nobody in their right mind would recommend that as a strategy.

So, in your pitch, it should be clear to your audience who your customer is and how you make money, even if it's as simple as "it's a SaaS product for inside sales managers." That tells us exactly who the customer is and exactly how the imaginary startup will make money (subscriptions).

## Who are you beholden to?

This lesson comes up a lot at Pitch Practice. The ensuing discussion usually works its way back to the Facebook example I mentioned earlier. Facebook has over 2 billion users, but they have thousands of customers (advertisers) who pay them money. Who is Facebook beholden to? Their *customers*.

When Facebook changes something in its UI or app or algorithm, that is most likely for the benefit of their advertisers.

Make sure that you can identify who your very specific, ideal, early customer segment is and that your audience is clear that you know *everything* about your customer.

**LESSON 11**: Make sure you can identify who your customer segment is and that you know everything about them.

**LESSON 12:** Traction rules. If you have 10 or 20 or 100 entities using (or paying for) your service, you must share that fact. If you have 10 customers, you're that much closer to product market fit.

# Chapter 10 - The Ask

## *"Be so good they can't ignore you." Steve Martin*

The last piece of the Pitch Practice structure of a great pitch is "the ask", and it's probably the second most difficult piece to get right. Most often, the problem statement is the hardest, but once you get that right, it doesn't change much unless you make a pivot. The "ask", however, might change every single time you say your pitch because your audience and your needs might change every time.

Gary Vaynerchuk calls it *"jab, jab, jab...right hook"* or *"give, give, give, give, ask."* We have to give value to our audience before we earn the right to ask for anything. That makes the ask in your pitch even harder and even more important. If you don't provide value to your audience, your "ask" will fall on deaf ears.

In every pitch, you have to ask for *something*, because at some point, as an entrepreneur, you're going to have to ask for money, either from a customer or an investor or both. So, you'd best get used to it, practice it, get comfortable with it, because it's not going away.

With that in mind, how do you know what to ask for? Here are some ideas.

- Ask for something you can control, if possible. If you're in an elevator with Sig Moseley, and you get the opportunity to say what you do, are you going to give him your card, or are you going to ask him for his? You ask him for his card and clearly ask his permission to call and set up the next meeting (the one and only goal of the elevator pitch).
- If you're raising money, that's your "ask". Own it, but be specific:
  - Say *exactly* how much money you are raising, and
  - Say *exactly* what you're going to do with that money.
  - These two points, in combination, demonstrate to investors that you've done your math.

- Knowing your audience is key. At Pitch Practice, the goal is to get better, which requires feedback on your pitch. That's an easy way to practice asking for something specific: "*I would really like your feedback on my pitch.*" See how easy that is?

- If you want the audience to do something, like download your app or follow you on Twitter, make it really easy for them to do it. It's at this point that you learn whether or not your Twitter handle or app name or website is easy to understand.

- If you're at an investor event, like Venture Atlanta, and the ask in your pitch is something like "Come by our booth", make it very specific, like "Please come to our booth number 1234 right in front of the Coffee Station".

- Remember that the audience, however large or small, has given you permission to speak. Asking your audience for something, after giving them value, makes it about them and not about you. Remember who the star of your show is. Hint: it's not you. It's your audience.

Adjust to your audience, particularly with your ask. When you pitch, you are almost always asking for something, even if it's "Vote for us to win!", so you should (a) know your audience before you pitch and (b) get very comfortable with asking for whatever it is you want from your audience. It might be referrals, advice, feedback, a vote, or if you're pitching investors, money! Ask for something you can control, whenever possible, but always, always ask for something.

**Every Startup Needs Something...Different**

You might not need to raise money, or you might not be ready to raise money yet. But that doesn't mean you don't need anything. What do you need?

- A co-founder
- Beta users
- A mentor
- An advisor
- A developer
- Customers
- Referrals
- A specific hire

Whatever you need, ask for it specifically. If you don't ask for it, you will never get it. And when you do ask for it, be very, very specific about that one thing that you're asking for.

In any pitch, very similar to a marketing landing page having a very clear Call To Action (CTA), you want to have a very clear ask. That means ask for one thing and one thing only. What do you need the most right now? Ask for it until you get it, then move on to what you need most then, and ask for it.

**LESSON 13**: Adjust your pitch to your audience, particularly with your ask. Know your audience before you pitch and get very comfortable with asking for whatever it is you want from your audience.

**LESSON 14:** When you say you're raising money, say an exact amount and say it with gusto: "We're raising $500k." You are never "looking to raise" money. You are "raising" X dollars to accomplish Y and Z, period. Own it.

# Chapter 11 - Tell Us A Story

*"The audience does not need to tune themselves to you. You need to tune your message to them. Skilled presenting requires you to understand their hearts and minds and create a message to resonate with what's already there." - Nancy Duarte*

We can draw more than just one point of inspiration from Simon Sinek's TED Talk and book, "Start with Why". One of the easiest methods of drawing in your audience to an understanding of you, your business, or your startup is to tell the story of why you are doing what you are doing.

- How did you discover the problem you're solving?
- How did you validate the problem in the marketplace?
- How did you come up with the solution?

- How did you get to the point of deciding, "Yes, I can start a business to do this"?
- How did you get your first customer?

Each of these is a story. To your audience, the best of which should be people in the market who are living the problem you're solving and people who have a financial stake if the problem can be solved, your story means the world!

A great example is New Story Charity, and, yes, the name fits as well. Brett Hagler had gone on a mission trip to Haiti after the 2010 earthquake had destroyed the homes of thousands of people there. He saw first hand what it was like to live in a cardboard tent with crime, disease, and starvation everywhere. That's how he learned of and validated the core problem. He also learned about the problem with the then current "solution" to the real problem.

The Red Cross, an international nonprofit with billions of dollars in resources, had built 6 homes there in 5 years, mainly due to the pure bureaucracy of the organization. Brett and his co-founders knew there had to be a better way to raise funds and build sustainable homes for families in Haiti and elsewhere. So they founded New Story, and built 100 homes in 100 days.

Telling a story makes everything better. There's a reason that fiction is so popular. People love a story, and when you're pitching a business, your story is about how the business came to be. The story of the problem you are determined to solve will hit home with your intended audience. Had Brett Hagler only heard about this problem and not experienced it first hand, his story would not be nearly as compelling.

(And, no, the fantastic use of the name "New *Story*" is not lost on me.)

Nancy Duarte's TED talk is a tremendous asset and guide about how to tell your story. Storytelling is not random. It's not made up. There's a scientifically based pattern for how to actually tell a compelling story, once you have one to tell. What is the story of how your startup came to be? Tell that story!

## Little Red Riding Hood

Do you know how old Little Red Riding Hood was? How old was her grandmother? What was in that basket? How big was the wolf? How far did the wolf track the girl? All these facts and figures don't matter, because you remember the *story*, not all the facts and stats. The same thing applies to your pitch. Your audience will remember a compelling story, but they will forget even the most astounding facts or statistics.

That doesn't mean you don't recite those facts that support your pitch, but you weave them into a story that everyone will remember.

**LESSON 15:** Telling a story makes everything better. There's a reason that fiction is so popular. People love a story, and when you're pitching a business, your story is about how the business came to be. The story of the problem you are determined to solve will hit home with your intended audience.

# Chapter 12 - Now Grow Your Elevator Pitch

*"One of the ways you convey the operational excellence is in the quality of the plan." - Marc Andreessen*

In an elevator pitch, you are it: your words, body language, timing, ask…everything. But if you're doing a pitch with a slide deck, that changes the dynamics of your presentation quite a bit. Here's one way to approach doing such a presentation, regardless of how long or short that presentation is.

Your slides are the cake. You are the icing. This is a fun way of saying that your slides should have little or no text at all ever, unless it's absolutely necessary. We have the interwebz, so you can find a picture to illustrate anything, or you can use Fiverr and pay someone a few bucks to create an image that illustrates your point. Then you tell the story behind that picture, much like Instagram: image first, then tell the story.

Are there exceptions to this "no text at all ever" rule? Sure, but that should be your starting point. When you are presenting, ask yourself one question:

### *Do you want the audience to have their eyes on you or on your slides?*

There are times when you want the audience to *really* see something on your slide. At those times, it is appropriate to be silent and allow your audience a moment to soak up whatever it is you want them to see. But at all other times, your slides are the cake, and you are the icing. They should be looking at you the entire time. For you, that means you must command their attention.

For your slides, it means that they must make a point very quickly, and then enable the audience to refocus back on you for the story or explanation behind that particular slide. Here are 4 points to go by when creating your slide deck for a presentation.

- A picture tells a thousand words
- People read at different speeds
- Text is boring, pictures rock

- Our brains process images faster than
  text

With these in mind, just as you can use the Pitch Practice structure as the very starting point for your elevator pitch, use the "no text at all ever" rule as the starting point for your pitch deck. Start with 0, and work from there. If you do have to add text, make sure it's brief and huge.

## Engage Your Audience During A Presentation

Giving an engaging presentation is hard work. Some people are natural orators, but most of us need practice, feedback, and guidance to improve our presenting skills. I used to teach the Digital Marketing class at General Assembly's Atlanta location, I still run the weekly Pitch Practice meetup of entrepreneurs every Friday in Atlanta, and I lead several other small groups of people in various other capacities.

Over the years, I've presented countless times to all types of people – investors, customers, employees, boards, students – and I've learned that there are five tactics that, used consistently, will help you keep any audience engaged.

1. **Ask questions** - Also known as the Socratic method, you teach by asking questions to the audience. Then you have instant material when you use the audience's answers in your talk. More importantly, asking questions gives you the ability to shine attention on different people in the room, which thoroughly engages those individuals. People love to tell their own story, so ask them open-ended questions about their experiences.

2. **Tell a story** - Tell stories that your audience can relate to. This means that you have to know your audience. Knowing your audience is part of your homework for any presentation, and it can help you not only with what questions to ask, but also with what kinds of stories you can tell that the audience will completely relate to. I recently led a seminar on blogging for your brand, and introduced myself by telling the audience that I began blogging 10 years ago when my wife and I traveled across the globe to adopt our two children. The response to that story was amazing.

3. **Use Humor** - This does not mean, "tell jokes." Unless you're a professional, telling jokes can be risky. Rather, use humor in telling your stories. Bring humor to your own mistakes, and your audience will instantly relate to your experiences.

4. **Move around** - If you are not behind a podium, move around the floor, so you can look different people in the eye. Eye contact is the first human connection we can have with another person. When you look someone in the eye, you are far more connected to them than if you don't look. To prove this point, try having a conversation with someone you know, and never look them in the eye. They will very clearly think that you are hiding something from them. The same concept applies to delivering a great presentation.

5. **Memorize Your Presentation** - Memorizing what you're going to say requires practice. When you're giving any presentation, you're selling yourself, so you should practice quite a lot before any presentation, big or small. I recommend practicing to the point of

memorization. When you stumble on words, your audience notices, whether you're really good at improvisation or not. When you deliver your words with confidence, no notes, and without looking at your slides (if you're using any), the audience perception is that you know the material and took the time to prepare. You took time for *them*.

When you prepare well for a presentation, you'll be more confident as you move around, look individuals in the eye, ask them questions, and tell humorous stories that the audience can relate to. These five simple tactics can make a huge difference in your ability to present yourself or your company to any audience.

**LESSON 16**: You have time for 5 slides in a 3-minute pitch. On average, most people talk for 2-3 minutes for each slide in a presentation. Having more slides does not make a better pitch.

**LESSON 17**: Video is prohibited, unless it's really, really freaking good. I've only seen video in a pitch work exactly one time. Be careful with video.

**LESSON 18**: Your slides are the cake. You are the icing. You can find a picture to illustrate anything, or use Fiverr and pay someone a few bucks to create an image that illustrates your point. Like Instagram: image first, then tell the story.

**LESSON 19:** If you're pitching in a contest, you would be wise to pay the $100 to get a pro to design your slides with as few words as possible and beautiful visuals. There's just no substitute for a great design.

# Chapter 13 - The Final Lesson

## *"Be yourself; everyone else is already taken." - Oscar Wilde*

Remember, good communication is consistent and repetitive. There are 6 items that you <u>must</u> include in your 30-second pitch:

1. Your name
2. Your company name
3. The problem
4. Your customer
5. Your solution
6. Your ask


It takes practice. However, you can memorize all the keywords and catchphrases you want to, and spit them out in an actual elevator or lengthy investor meeting, but that won't get you to the next level. But here's the advice that will.

Are you ready for it? Because it's not easy. Here goes.

# Be yourself.

Not what you wanted to hear, is it? You have to be yourself. When you're pitching a startup with no working product, no paying customers, and no revenue, guess what the investors are buying? <u>You</u>.

So, deliver all the fancy memorized canned pitches you want, but don't think that one perfectly delivered 3-minute / 4 slide presentation is going to land you a sweet seed round. You have to be so familiar and comfortable with your product, your space, your economics, your competitors, your process, and your future that it's part of who you are and how you speak.

The goal of the elevator pitch is to get to the next meeting, and you won't have a script. You'll have to rely on your ability to be yourself.

**LESSON 20:** When the startup is just the idea, YOU are 100% of the startup, and anyone who believes in the startup is believing in you. Be yourself.

# Conclusion

## *"Be nice. Dream Big. Work hard, play hard. Pay it forward." - David Cummings, Founder of Atlanta Tech Village*

I owe a huge shout out to the great folks at Atlanta Tech Village for allowing, tolerating, then enabling, and now promoting this weekly meetup for entrepreneurs. Thank you very much! And, as we say at every session, it would be pretty boring if everybody came to observe and nobody pitched, so HOORAH to everyone who has ever pitched at Pitch Practice!

People new to Pitch Practice ask me often, "why do you start this?" Many think I'm some sort of pitch guru or something. Far from the truth. I've always been comfortable speaking in public, but have never attended Toastmasters or any other speaker training. I started Pitch Practice because the folks at ATDC offered Pitch Gauntlet once a month at 7 am on Tuesdays. I needed more.

So, apparently, do a few thousand or so other people. I started Pitch Practice as a way to serve, and to fill a need in the community, and I've learned far more from every session than anyone else. I learn something new every time.

Thank you.

**LESSON 21:** Start something that benefits someone else. You'll be glad you did.

# APPENDIX: The 21 Lessons

1.  Solve a problem, even if it's just for you at the beginning. You never know who it will help.

2.  Be consistent. Show up prepared every time. Because you just never know.

3.  To overcome your weaknesses, find a way to serve other people as you build those weaknesses into strengths. That's all Pitch Practice ever was or is: a way for me to serve other entrepreneurs by using my strengths and experience. You have strengths and experience, too.

4.  Having a construct in which to create your pitch is crucial. Just like when you start a business, you need some boundaries, a business model, something upon which to base how you go about everything on a day to day basis, you need a place to start and some boundaries around your pitch.

5.  You really don't need 30 seconds to get your message across. We use 30 seconds as an arbitrary tool for building discipline into your words about what it is that you do. Set your

own bar for excellence, then practice and beat it.

6.  If you have deep domain expertise, say it! That means you've lived this problem, and you understand who it affects the results of fixing that problem. It means you have credibility.

7.  Anyone can steal your idea. Nobody can steal your execution. So, share your idea. Someone already has stolen it! They just call it something different and you don't know about it yet. If you have to get an NDA from everyone you talk to, you're doomed from the start.

8.  The problem is the pain in a market space. Your solution is what you do to solve it. You must know the difference.

9.  You have competition. Don't ever say "we have no competition" anywhere in your pitch, or anywhere else for that matter. Your biggest competitor is status quo, and getting people to change the way they do things is incredibly hard. If you really, actually don't have any competition, you have discovered something

far bigger than you know, or there is no market for other competitors to enter.

10. If there's a simple analogy you can use (e.g., "match.com for networking"), use it. Sometimes that's what makes it clear or real for your audience. However, be careful using "Uber for _____." That can backfire on you in a hurry.

11. Make sure you can identify who your customer segment is and that you know everything about them.

12. Traction rules. If you have 10 or 20 or 100 entities using (or paying for) your service, you must share that fact. If you have 10 customers, you're that much closer to product market fit.

13. Adjust your pitch to your audience, particularly with your ask. Know your audience before you pitch and get very comfortable with asking for whatever it is you want from your audience.

14. When you say you're raising money, say an exact amount and say it with gusto: "We're raising $500k." You are never "looking to

raise" money. You are "raising" X dollars to accomplish Y and Z, period. Own it.

15. Telling a story makes everything better. There's a reason that fiction is so popular. People love a story, and when you're pitching a business, your story is about how the business came to be. The story of the problem you are determined to solve will hit home with your intended audience.

16. You have time for 5 slides in a 3-minute pitch. On average, most people talk for 2-3 minutes for each slide in a presentation. Having more slides does not make a better pitch.

17. Video is prohibited, unless it's really, really freaking good. I've only seen video in a pitch work exactly one time. Be careful with video.

18. Your slides are the cake. You are the icing. You can find a picture to illustrate anything, or use Fiverr and pay someone a few bucks to create an image that illustrates your point. Like Instagram: image first, then tell the story.

19. If you're pitching in a contest, you would be wise to pay the $100 to get a pro to design

your slides with as few words as possible and beautiful visuals. There's just no substitute for a great design.

20. When the startup is just the idea, YOU are 100% of the startup, and anyone who believes in the startup is believing in you. Be yourself.

21. Start something that benefits someone else. You'll be glad you did.

Made in the USA
Columbia, SC
28 January 2021

31782683R00067